Un
STOPPABLE

*Possibility Thinking That Breaks Barriers, Keeps You
Focused, and Thrives Through Storms*

Bishop Dr. Mark Kariuki

Unstoppable
by Bishop Dr. Mark Kariuki
Copyright ©2025 Bishop Dr. Mark Kariuki

ISBN 978-1-63360-344-8

All rights reserved. This book is protected under the copyright laws of the United States of America. This book may not be copied or reprinted for com-mercial gain or profit.

Scripture quotations are taken from the King James Version and rest in the public domain.

        For Worldwide Distribution   Printed in the USA

Urban Press
PO Box 5044
Williamsburg, VA 23188
+1.757.808.5776
www.urbanpress.us

Table of Contents

Preface	4
PART I THE POSSIBILITY MINDSET	9
1 For With God All Things Are Possible	10
2 The Unbreakable Partnership	19
3 When I Chose to Believe Anyway	21
4 I Jumped Anyway	24
5 I Grew Up Hearing It	27
6 Stranded but Not Forsaken	31
7 Faith at 30,000 Feet	40
8 Faith That Waited	53
9 The Reception of Relentless Faith	71
10 The Plot We Prayed For	75
11 Benches of Faith, Trucks of Favour	79
12 The Exodus	84

13
One Metre, One Family, One Vision 92

14
The Battle Within 96

15
Renewing the Mind to Walk in Abundance 100

16
Redeemed from The Thorns 104

17
The Time to Sow, The Life to Reap 108

18
The Gift That Multiplies 113

19
From Empty Pockets to Full Purpose 117

20
The Orange That Preached Back to Me 120

21
The Seed Always Knows What to Do 126

PART II
UNSTOPPABLE IN THE STORM 131

22
Unstoppable in the Storm 132

23
God Will Supply The Potatoes We Never Planted 137

24
When Influence Does Not Distract the Called 141

25
What God Thinks of Me Is Enough 145

26
Anchored in the Storm (When the Fire
    Finds You)   149

PART III
THE FUEL THAT KEEPS YOU GOING   153
    (BONUS SECTION)

About the Author   177

Preface

I did not write this pocket-sized book from the comfort of ease but from the furnace of real life. UNSTOPPABLE is not a theory, it is a testimony. It is forged from moments of victory and valleys of loss. From standing on mountain tops in full view of God's glory to walking through storms where the only thing I had left to hold onto was His Word.

In over four decades of ministry, I have learned three essential truths. First, life does not give you a free pass because you are a believer. Second, faith does not exempt you from storms but equips you to outlast them. And finally, purpose is not the absence of pressure but the force that keeps you moving through it.

I have buried loved ones, stood before congregations with a broken heart, and faced seasons I did not expect. Yet in every chapter of my life, I have seen one constant: *the faithfulness of God and the unstoppable power of a mind fixed on possibility.*

This book is not just for pastors or church leaders. It is for anyone who has ever been told, *"You cannot."* It is for the dreamer who has hit a wall. For the young person fighting discouragement. For the entrepreneur navigating uncertainty. For the parent holding on through tears. It is for you who still believe that there is more ahead, and refuse to give up now.

UNSTOPPABLE is a guide to developing the mindset that sees light when others see darkness. It will help you embrace possibility where others see limitation, remain steady when life grows chaotic, and protect the fire within you when the winds of adversity rise. What I share in these pages has carried me through some of life's fiercest trials. These principles are grounded, proven, and full of life; they are truths that uplift, sustain, and empower.

Read with an open heart. Read with expectation. And as you turn these pages, may your faith be reignited, your focus sharpened, and your steps redirected towards a future filled with purpose, clarity, and victory.

Because no matter the storm, no matter the odds, you were never built to break. You were born to be **UNSTOPPABLE**.

Bishop Dr. Mark Kariuki

www.markkariuki.org

Part I
THE POSSIBILITY MINDSET

1

For With God All Things Are Possible

Before we can talk about possibility thinking, before we start climbing mountains or breaking through barriers, there is something we must settle in our hearts once and for all. We must know God. I am not speaking about hearing His name on Sundays. I am not talking about what people say about Him. I mean truly knowing who He is.

You see, if you do not know who God is, that powerful declaration, For With God All Things Are Possible, will just sit on your lips and never reach your heart. It will be like a powerful key held in the hand of someone who has never seen a door. But when you come to know Him, truly know Him, something changes. You shift from doubt to faith, from hesitation to boldness, from questions to confidence.

Let me tell you who God is. He is the Creator of the heavens and the earth. He spoke, and galaxies obeyed. He breathed, and man became a living being. He commands the wind, and it listens. He owns everything. There is nothing, I repeat, nothing outside His reach.

You may be thinking, *that sounds good, Bishop, but is He really able to do something in my situation?* Oh, yes! He is able. That is why I love what Paul wrote to the Ephesians in Ephesians 3:20, *"Now unto Him who is able to do exceedingly abundantly above all that we ask or think, according to the power that works in us."* That is not just Scripture to be quoted, that is a revelation to be lived!

This is the God I preach. The God of exceedingly. The God of abundantly. The God of above. He does not just answer prayer, He goes beyond the prayer. He does not stop at what you imagined, He exceeds what your mind could put together. That is why I know that no barrier can stop you. No storm can finish you. No distraction can steal your focus, not when your thinking is rooted in Him.

You were not born to give up. You were not created to run and hide. You are meant to rise. You are built to thrive. You are wired for more, because you are connected to the God of more. **You are UNSTOPPABLE!**

Stay with me as we walk together through this journey of possibility thinking, the kind that refuses to bow, the kind that pushes through, the kind that brings down walls and opens doors.

Now when you know God, and you know His ability, then it is also important to know His availability. Is He available? Are there times when He is absent? Yet He says, and I believe it without doubt, *I will never leave you nor forsake you.* He says, *I will be with you always, even to the end of time.* That is not a casual promise. That is an eternal assurance from the One who cannot lie.

Now when you capture that He is able, and He is available, and He has all the power, then the next thing becomes very clear. You must now look and ask, "*How does He operate?*" How does this God who is able to do exceedingly abundantly above all that we ask or think actually work? What is His pattern? What is His method? This is where your eyes are opened to a powerful truth. He operates by saying. Yes, He works by declaring. He functions through speaking. The way to understand how God operates is by going back to the beginning. Go to Genesis 1:1-31 (KJV), you will see it clearly. In the King James Version, about nine times, it is written, *And God said.* Not once. Not twice. Over and over again.

And God said. That was the pattern. That was the movement. That was the release of power. So, God operates by saying.

Now when we realise that He operates by saying, then we begin to understand that the Word carries weight. It carries authority. It carries creative power. The Word is not just information. It is action. It is life. When the Scripture declares, *For with God All Things Are Possible*, it is not an empty statement. It is a divine reality. It simply means this, as long as you are walking with God, as long as you allow God to say, as long as you let His Word find expression in your life, then nothing is going to be impossible. The barriers will give way. The doors will open. The storm will bow. Because when God speaks, everything listens.

But this brings a question. A question many people quietly carry in their hearts. If God lives in heaven, when is He going to speak? If He speaks through prophets, and prophets are not always around, then how shall I hear His voice? This is where many lose their way. This is where confusion enters. Because of that misunderstanding, people begin to chase after voices. They go looking for prophets. They ask strangers, "What *is God saying about* me?" They plead, "Say *something. Give me a* word." And often, they end up walking in uncertainty, not because God is silent, but because they do not know where He is speaking from.

Remember what Jesus said in **Revelation 3:20**: *"Behold, I stand at the door and knock. If anyone hears My voice and opens the door, I will come in and eat with him, and he with Me."* These are not just nice words; they are real. Jesus is always ready to come into our lives, but He waits for us to open the door. When we invite Him in, He comes to stay and be close to us.

Then He said something even deeper. *My Father and I will come in and make our home within you.* So where is God speaking from? He is not shouting from the sky. He is not hidden behind the clouds. He is not waiting in some faraway corner of the universe. He is right here. Inside you. Speaking from within. Speaking through His Word. Speaking through that quiet nudge, that inner witness, that unshakeable conviction.

So, this statement *"For with God all things are possible"*, will benefit you if you understand all that I have mentioned because now you can say with full assurance that the moment you got born again, something powerful happened. Not just a change in your name. Not just a shift in your lifestyle. No, something greater than that took place.

The moment I got born again, God the Father, God the Son, and God the Holy Spirit came and made their home in me. I became their dwelling place. I became the address of heaven on earth. That is not just a theological idea. This is a divine reality.

And because I have become their dwelling place, something else becomes clear. If God wants to speak, He will use my mouth. If God wants to bless, He will use my hands. If He wants to comfort, He will use my heart. If He wants to walk into a place, He will use my feet. Now you know how God operates. He operates by saying. That changes everything.

And that gives me confidence. That builds my faith. That fuels my courage. Because now, when I speak anything in alignment with His Word, it will come to pass. Not maybe. Not someday. It will come to pass. Because He still operates by saying.

Therefore, I refuse to speak defeat. I refuse to speak fear. I refuse to speak limitation. My words are no longer empty echoes. My words are channels. My words are carriers. They carry the same life that created the heavens and the earth.

2

The Unbreakable Partnership

A lot of people read the Scripture and understand it to mean that by God, all things are possible, that when something is done by God alone, then it is possible. But that is not what it says. The Scripture says, with God.

That changes everything.

With God means partnership. It means cooperation. It means alignment. It means you and God, walking together, speaking together, acting together. When you and God come into agreement, when your heart says yes to His will, when your words echo His Word, then all things become possible.

It is not God acting alone, and it is not you trying alone. It is you and God together. That is the power of with God.

And that is where Matthew 18:19 backs it up. It says, *If two of you shall agree on earth as touching anything that they shall ask, it shall be done for them of my Father which is in heaven.*

Agreement is powerful. When you and God agree, there is nothing that will be impossible. When your voice joins His voice, and your faith leans on His Word, the impossible bows. Mountains move. Closed doors open. Delays break. All things are possible with God.

3

When I Chose to Believe Anyway

There are many moments I could share with you. Many turning points. Many crossroad decisions. But one of them stands out so clearly in my mind that it feels like it happened just yesterday. I had just completed Form Four, and I had one dream in my heart, and that was to join the army and become an officer cadet.

Now, this was not just a passing thought. It was a serious desire. I had been trained in Form Three. I had the physical strength. I had the stamina. I knew I qualified physically. All I needed was to secure a second division in my results, and I would be good to go.

When the time came, we reported to Lanet Barracks in Nakuru for the recruitment. There were about one hundred and six of us. The officers made it very clear that this was not a walk in the park. For one whole week, we went through obstacles, tests, drills, and elimination exercises. Each day ended with a roll call. Every evening, some names would be called out, and just like that, they would be told to pack up and go home. No questions. No discussion. If you missed the mark, you were out.

And then came one particular test that shook me. A swimming test.

Now, let me confess right here, I did not know how to swim. Not then. Not now. And the requirement was simple. You had to dive into the swimming pool from the deep end. Not from the shallow side. From the deep end. That was the task.

So here I am, sitting at the edge, watching as one after another is called out.

"So and so, are you going to jump?"

"No."

"Go home."

Next one.

"Are you going to jump?"

"Yes."

And those who could swim would dive confidently. Some would take off like torpedoes, cutting through the water. Others just jumped like they were diving into a pit in the shamba. But they jumped.

Now I am sitting there thinking. I want to join the army. I have passed all the other tests. But now this? What do I do when my name is called? I am weighing my fear against my desire. My doubt against my dream. My limitations against my calling.

And right there, in that moment, I had to decide.

4

I Jumped Anyway

So, when they called my name, I had to make a decision.

And I said to myself, *"Well, I will jump."*

Yes, I will jump, not because I knew how to swim, but because I believed they could not have brought me all the way here just to let me die in a swimming pool. I told myself, if I do not swim, surely someone will rescue me. And as I looked more closely, I saw that there were people already inside the pool. That gave me some courage. That gave me a kind of confidence that told me, *"You will not drown. You will go through this."*

So, when they called my name, I stepped forward and jumped into the deep end.

Eyes closed. Body tight. Everything inside me tensed. And I felt myself going down. Down. Down. Deeper. Down. Then I touched the bottom. My feet hit the floor of the pool. And then, slowly, I started rising.

That moment right there, that jump, was a possibility decision. A moment where I chose to believe, even when everything else inside me said, *"You cannot do this."*

I may not have made it to the end of that recruitment. I may not have qualified to be a soldier in the national army. But that day, I passed a personal test. A test of courage. A test of faith. A test of obedience to a deep inner voice that said, *"You must jump."*

And that is why today I am not wearing boots and carrying a rifle.

Instead, I stand before you wearing the full armour of God. I may not have joined the army that I had my eyes on, but I joined a greater army — the army of the Lord. I became a soldier of the Most High. Not by accident. But by calling.

Sometimes the jump is not about where you land. Sometimes the jump is about proving to yourself that fear will not hold you hostage. That doubt will not control your destiny. That impossibility is not your language.

5

I Grew Up Hearing It

I grew up hearing my mother. A woman of faith. A woman of deep conviction. My mother did not go to Bible school, but her theology was fireproof. She would say it over and over again, *"There is nothing that is too difficult for God. There is nothing that is too hard for Him."*

And she said it in a firm voice. Not with uncertainty, but with a settled assurance. So, I grew up knowing that indeed, there is nothing that is too hard for God. Whether I saw Him or I did not see Him. Whether I felt Him or I did not feel Him. Whether the door opened immediately or not. That did not matter. What I knew was this, there is nothing too hard for God.

Now, I can tell you many stories. Many, many, many. My life is full of those stories. Possibility stories. Stories that may look small to some but were defining for me. Let me take you back to my student days.

We had this burning passion to go on missions. We wanted to preach. We wanted to see souls saved. We wanted to shake the gates of hell with our praise. The only problem was this, we had no money. Nothing. Not even for fare. But we had faith.

So, what do you do when you have no fare, but you have fire in your heart? We chose the road.

We would gather, agree on the mission destination, maybe it was a high school somewhere and then we would head to the roadside. We would start singing. We would start dancing. Right there by the roadside. Not in a church. Not on a stage. Just right there. And any vehicle coming, whether it was a matatu, a lorry, or even a tractor we would raise our hands and hitchhike.

Sometimes someone would stop and say, *"Hop in, I can take you a few miles."* We would jump in, bless them, sing some more, and then alight when they reached their turn-off. Then we would repeat the same. Dance again. Sing again. Until another vehicle came.

Sometimes we would use four different vehicles to reach our destination. Sometimes one person would be so excited to carry us all the way to the meeting, and we would arrive like VIPs, only that our shoes had more dust than polish.

But we always got there.

Why? Because we trusted. We trusted that what we were doing was not for ourselves. We were not chasing our own ambitions. We were doing it for God. We were moving in obedience. We were on divine assignment.

And when you are on divine assignment, doors open. Paths clear. Favour locates you. Help comes. And God shows up in ways no one can explain.

So, I never sat down and said, *"It is not possible."*

No. I got up. I believed. And I went.

6

Stranded but Not Forsaken

There's this particular mission. I led many years ago to a place called Duruma Land, nestled in the heart of Kenya's coastal county of Kwale. Tucked away beyond the busy towns and into the serene countryside, this region is home to the vibrant Duruma community, a people rich in culture, hospitality, and deep spiritual hunger.

I remember it vividly, not just because of where we were going, but because of what happened on that trip.

I was leading a team of passionate young people, the youth and the choir. We had prayed. We had fasted. We were ready to take the gospel to Nduruma. It was a weekend mission, and our then-pastor entrusted me with the transport money for the entire group. He placed it in my hand with confidence. And I took that responsibility seriously.

We boarded a matatu, and just before we took off, the conductor and the driver insisted we pay *all* the fare in advance, both for the trip to Nduruma and for the return on Sunday. I did not hesitate. I believed them. I had no reason to doubt. They looked honest. Their words sounded sure. So, I handed over all the money fare to and from Nduruma, in full. They assured me that they would drop us off on Friday, and return promptly to pick us up on Sunday at exactly 12 noon.

I trusted their word.

They dropped us on Friday as promised. We held a powerful outreach on Saturday. There was singing, preaching, dancing, and more importantly, people gave their lives to Christ.

Sunday came, and we prepared for the final service. But in the back of my mind, I kept watching the time. I knew we had to be done by 12 noon because the matatu was supposed to arrive at that exact hour. I did not want to keep the driver waiting.

So, we hurried through the Sunday service. We ended right on time. 12 noon sharp. We gathered our bags. We waited.

But the matatu never came.

12:15. Nothing. 12:30. Silence. One o'clock. Still nothing. And I had paid them every single shilling before we even reached Nduruma. I gave it because I trusted. I believed. I did not hold back or second-guess the arrangement.

We waited.

Two in the afternoon. No matatu.

3 o'clock. Still nothing.

7 p.m. nightfall had fully draped itself over Nduruma.

8 p.m.- darkness thick as a blanket, and still, no sign of the vehicle.

Now the murmuring began. The team I had led, the youth, the choir, and the faithful who had danced and sung with joy the day before, were now anxious and frustrated. And rightly so. It was Sunday evening in the middle of Nduruma Land, far from the familiar comforts of home, tucked deep in the rural edges of Arusha. And by Monday morning, most of us were expected back at work in Mombasa.

The questions started flying.

"Why did you pay them all the money?"
"We should have just paid half!"

"Let's start walking. Maybe we'll find another ride."

"This was a bad idea."

I understood their frustration. I felt the weight of leadership settle heavily on my shoulders. But I also knew one thing for sure, we were not going to walk in the dark. Not through Nduruma. Not with the sisters in our group, some of whom were in heels. And not with a river between us and the nearest town... a river with no bridge, only shallow waters we had to wade through, guided only by daylight.

So, I spoke up.

"No. We'll not walk in the night. We'll wait here. If nothing happens by morning, we'll rise at 5 a.m. and cross together."

That settled it, not entirely peacefully, but at least the group agreed. We stayed, holding onto hope, praying in our hearts, and waiting on a

God I had always believed was never late.

And then... just past midnight... we saw it.

A faint light flickering from a distance. It grew closer. Brighter. Headlights! You would think heaven had just opened its gates.

Cheers erupted. People hugged. Some laughed. Others nearly cried. It was *our* matatu!

The driver told us what had happened, the vehicle had broken down right after they dropped us off. They had spent the entire Sunday repairing it. No phones, no way to reach us. Only after everything was fixed did they start the long journey back.

We boarded with joy, exhausted but relieved. We rode through the rest of the night, arriving in Mombasa just as the first light of morning touched the coastal skyline. No time for sleep.

We rushed home, took quick showers, changed clothes, and went straight to work.

Looking back now, I smile.

Because I learned something again that night, something I have known deep down since I was a boy watching my mother speak faith into every impossibility:

With God, all things are possible.

You know, there are those moments in life when people do not just lose patience; they nearly lose faith in you altogether. The kind of moments where the easiest thing would be to stone the leader, question their integrity, or whisper among themselves, *"Maybe he struck a deal with the makanga... maybe he kept a cut and left us stranded."*

And honestly? I would not blame them. That is how frustration talks. That is how fear speaks when you are in the middle of nowhere, and hope feels delayed.

But through it all, my confidence remained anchored in God.

I knew why we came.

We did not come for a trip.

We did not come for money or applause.

We came to **preach**. And we had seen **God move**. We had seen Him touch hearts, save souls, and lift spirits.

And in that, I rested.

That is why even when everything in the natural said we were stuck, I believed He would make a way. And true to His nature, He did.

There have been many such moments in my journey. Moments when doors opened that no man could explain. Moments where logic gave way to grace and impossibility bowed to faith.

I have walked through valleys with no roadmap, led missions with no budget, and seen provision show up in the most unexpected of ways, not because I had a perfect plan but because I trusted a perfect God.

So yes, I have lived it. I have seen it. I have walked it.

With God, all things are possible.

Because once you begin to walk with the God of possibilities, you discover...

The journey never stops.

7

Faith at 30,000 Feet

This happened not too long ago.

We were on the runway, the engines roaring with maximum thrust, just about to take off for our destination, Kisumu. As we hurtled down the tarmac, slicing through the morning air, I suddenly heard it.

A sharp pop.

Loud. Violent. Unmistakable.

It came from the outer side of the window, on the very side where I was seated.

Now, as someone who has been behind the wheel for years, there are things your instincts pick up before your brain even processes them.

That sound? It was not ordinary. Something told me *that wasn't just turbulence, that wasn't just wind.*

I sat up and leaned slightly, peering towards the wing. I thought surely the pilot would hit the brakes, call it off, abort the take-off.

He pushed on.

The aircraft lifted, yes, but you could feel it. This bird was not soaring; it was *struggling*. The ascent was sluggish, almost reluctant, as though the plane was battling against an invisible resistance.

Now, I have flown this route more times than I can count. I know the rhythm, the pitch of the engines, the tempo of the climb. But this time? The harmony was off. One engine was singing; the other, suspiciously quiet.

What was more unsettling was not just the sound or lack thereof but the silence that followed.

No word from the captain.

No reassurances from the cabin crew.

Just a cabin full of passengers exchanging uneasy glances, each one running their own private simulation of what might be going wrong.

We climbed. Slowly. Painfully. Then levelled.

Only then, when the tension had fermented into pure, silent anxiety, did the captain's voice finally crackle through the speaker.

"Ladies and gentlemen, this is your captain speaking. We have unfortunately lost one engine..."

My friend, the air in that cabin changed instantly.

This was no longer just a flight, it became a prayer meeting.

You could see it in people's eyes. You could feel it in the breath being held.

The ground below? Not as far as you would like.

The sky above? Not as comforting as before.

Right next to me sat a man who had, up to this point, been quietly minding his business. But now? His body language betrayed him completely. He was visibly shaken, rubbing his hands together, glancing out the window, brushing his forehead, and tapping his leg.

Finally, he turned to me and said, in a voice barely louder than a whisper.

"Excuse me... Do you think everything is all right with this plane?"

Now I had to make a decision.

You see, I have read the Scriptures. And I know this truth *"Every matter shall be established by the testimony of two or three witnesses."* So here I am, seated in a plane that has just lost an engine.

And here is this man, nervous, shaken, hoping that I would agree with his fear and establish with him that something is wrong.

But deep within me, I knew I carried something greater. I knew I had a word. I had a mission. I had a destiny.

So, I looked at him and said calmly, *"Everything is okay."* Because the moment I agreed with him that it *wasn't* okay, we would have established that fear. And I was not about to plant my faith in fear.

I did not board that plane to die.

I boarded it to reach my next destination.

I am on assignment. I am unstoppable until I accomplish what I was born to do.

You could see how troubled he was. He kept trying to wave down the flight attendants, his voice growing more urgent *"Are we okay? Are we okay? I'm concerned!"*

But the crew could not come; they too were strapped in, seatbelt signs still glowing above our heads. Regulations.

He turned to me again and asked, *"Have you ever been in something like this before?"*

I smiled slightly and said, *"Oh yes. Several times."*

I told him about the time we were about to land in Nairobi, and suddenly, just as we were touching down, the pilot pulled the plane back up sharply. No explanation. No warning. Just up again, into the skies.

Later, they told us there was heavy fog and zero visibility, so they could not land. We circled and circled, and when the fog did not clear, we were diverted to Mombasa. We landed safely there, did not even disembark, and as soon as we got the green light, we flew back to Nairobi and landed without incident. Everyone got home safely.

"Are you sure this one will land well?" he asked, still wringing his hands.

"Yes," I told him firmly. *"We will land well."*

Because walking with God teaches you to acknowledge the situation. Yes, we have lost an engine, *but to see it through the lens of faith*. And when you see from God's perspective, you do not panic. You do not make agreements with fear.

You rest. You trust. You believe. That is how you see God working in your life, not just in good times but in crises too.

Meanwhile, our plane kept circling round and round the Ngong Hills. Over and over again, I would look down and see the same hill come back into view. Four, maybe five times we looped, waiting for clearance to land. All this time, we were still on just one engine, the pilot and co-pilot working hard to stabilise and manoeuvre the aircraft.

You start to wonder, is it the plane that is hesitant to land? Or are the skies just not ready for us yet?

In line with the phrase that *"with God, all things are possible"*, many thoughts crossed my mind up there in the sky. First, I remembered the Scripture, *"It is appointed for man to die once, and after that comes judgment."*

Then another truth came, *"The secret things belong to the Lord our God."*

Among those secret things are when we shall die, how we shall die, and where we shall die.

So, there I was, thousands of feet above sea level, circling the Ngong Hills, with only one functioning engine on a plane that was designed to fly with two. And I found myself wondering, *"Could this be the way God ordained for me to transition?"*

But then I remembered *death is not final.* Death is a doorway. A passage into the other world. A divine transition.

So, I sat quietly and searched my soul. *"Is there anyone I've offended and never made things right with?*

Is there anyone I hold bitterness against?

Is there any unfinished business between me and man or me and God?"

And the answer that came brought peace.

There was none.

No lingering bitterness, no unresolved offence.

And so, I rested in that peace. Because if this was to be the moment I would meet my Maker, then I was ready.

As the plane circled again, I looked out the window and saw the same Ngong Hills again and again. Each time we looped, that familiar silhouette of the hills returned. And I could not help but remember the tragic stories of others who perished in plane crashes right over those hills. I wondered quietly, *"Is this how it ends? Will our aircraft collide with one of these ridges?"*

You see, we were not flying very high; the plane had lost height, and the proximity to the rugged terrain outside was unsettling.

You see the hills.

Then you pass them.

Then you see them again.

And again.

And again.

But amid those loops and spiralling thoughts, one truth anchored me.

With God, all things are possible.

That truth became my lifeline.

My focus shifted from fear to faith.

From uncertainty to unwavering trust.

And eventually, clearance came, and we landed.

Safely.

Miraculously.

There was no crash. No tragedy. No death.

We moved to the lounge, and they informed us that they had secured another aircraft scheduled to leave at noon. But I had a meeting in Kisumu at 10 a.m. That ship had sailed.

So, I called the regional overseers in Kisumu.

I said, *"Go ahead with the meeting. I won't make it today."*

I canceled the flight.

The rest of the passengers went on with the journey and touched down safely, including a man from Kisii I had met earlier. He had just arrived from the U.S. and was heading for a burial. We had met in the terminal, and he had told me he used to watch me on TV before moving to America. We exchanged contacts.

Later that day, he called me. *"We have landed,"* he said. *"Everything went well."* And that is how I knew *God had carried them through.*

Just a testimony of God's mercy, God's timing, and the power of holding onto faith when the sky seems uncertain.

I did not travel that day, but I knew the hand of God had been present, guiding the pilot, calming my heart, and using that delay to remind me. *Every step we take, every place we go, if God is with us, we are never really off course. We are simply on divine timing.*

8

Faith That Waited

In the early years of ministry, we held our services at the Old Town Hall in Nakuru town. We rented that hall for eight years. It became our place of prayer, our sanctuary, and for quite some time, we were comfortable there. We did not feel the urgency to seek our own place. It served our needs until it no longer did.

As time passed, our congregation began to grow significantly. What was once spacious became cramped. Then came the unsettling pressure from the city council. Some officials began to murmur that we had turned a public facility, a city council hall, into a church. They insisted on reclaiming the space, expressing their intention to rent it out to someone else. That was the point at which our eyes opened. We realised we could no longer rely on temporary accommodation. It was time to pursue our own land, our own sanctuary.

So, we began the search. One day, someone approached me and informed me of a piece of land whose lease had expired. They said I could apply for it. I asked, *"Is it legal?"* and they confirmed that it was. I responded, *"As long as I am not stealing from anyone and everything is in order, I will apply."*

Now, in those days, land applications of that nature could only be approved by one person, the late President Daniel Toroitich arap Moi. At that time, I did not know him personally, and he certainly did not know me. I was not on television then. I was just a local preacher known around Nakuru. But word had gone out that *"If you want to get healed, go to Pastor Mark's place."*

People came to the Old Town Hall for prayers. Those who could not make it there came directly to my house in Langa Langa Mwisho. I had prayed for many people in that area, but the president was not one of them, and I had no direct line to him.

So, I asked myself, *if I write this application letter, how will it ever reach him?* Then it struck me. The President had a chapel at his Kabarak residence, and that chapel had a chaplain, Reverend Kareli. I thought to myself, *Reverend Kareli is called by God. I am also called by God. That means our boss is one and the same.*

That became my conviction. That was my open door.

I decided that I would approach him not as a stranger but as a fellow servant in the Lord's vineyard. He may have been the chaplain to the president, while I was the pastor to the ordinary *mwananchi,* the common people, but the calling was from the same Master. Our assignments were different, but our divine employer was the same, our Heavenly Father.

So, one day I looked for his telephone number. Somebody gave it to me, and in my house, I had a telephone. I picked up the receiver and called Kabarak High School. I said, *"My name is Reverend Mark Kariuki. May I speak to Reverend Kareli?"*

Now, these are the kinds of calls where you are told to wait while they go to look for the person. So, I stood there, holding the receiver, listening to the stillness on the other end as they went to find him. After a short while, someone returned and told me, *"He is in class. Could you call again after this lesson?"*

I said, *"Alright."* I waited and called again at the suggested time. I introduced myself once more. This time, Reverend Kareli came to the telephone. He answered, *"Hello, Reverend."*

He did not know who this Reverend Mark Kariuki was, but one thing I knew was this. He knew the Boss. And I also knew the Boss. Our Heavenly Father had called us both. That was all the introduction I needed.

I told him, *"My name is Reverend Mark Kariuki. We worship at the Old Town Hall in Nakuru, and I would like to have a meeting with you. When are you coming to town?"*

He said, *"I will be coming to town tomorrow. Where would you like us to meet?"*

I replied, *"Can we meet at the Rift Valley Sports Club?"*

The truth is, I was not a member of that sports club. However, I knew some members of our church who were registered there. I reached out to one of them and made arrangements. That church member accompanied me and helped me gain access to the club.

I had chosen that location with care. The sports club was an open and relaxed environment. I sensed that he would be more comfortable meeting there than in a busy or more exposed location.

By the time we met, I had already written a letter. I folded it carefully and placed it in my pocket. It was addressed to the President because I knew that only he could authorise the allocation of that land. I had anticipated that Reverend Kareli might tell me to write a letter that he would deliver to the President, so I came ready.

When we met, I greeted him and shared the full story. I explained who we were, where we worshiped, and why we were looking for land.

I told him that we had identified a specific piece of land, whose lease had expired. I explained that the land had two title deeds. One of them had been renewed, but the other, the one not in use, had not. That was the portion we were interested in.

He asked me, *"Are you sure about that?"*

I said, *"Yes, I am."*

He asked, *"What do you want to use the land for?"*

I answered, *"To build a church."*

He replied, *"Alright, as long as it is not your personal land. If it is for the church, I shall take the letter."*

He then continued, *"What you need to do is go and write a letter. Say what you need to say. State clearly the details. Then give it to me, and I will take it."*

I smiled and said, *"I have already written the letter. I brought it with me."*

I reached into my pocket and handed it to him. He unfolded it, read through it quietly, then looked at me and said, *"This is good. I will take it."*

And just like that, he took the letter and left.

I was filled with hope. I believed that everything had fallen into place. I expected to be called that very Sunday. I waited.

And then I waited.

And waited.

And waited again.

Each day came and went without a word. Still, I waited.

Eventually, my patience was stirred. I felt compelled to follow up. So, I picked up the telephone and called Reverend Kareli. I asked him whether he had delivered the letter.

He said, *"No, no, I gave it. I gave the letter to the President. Let's just wait."*

Now, this was one of those moments in life where you have no room to push, no room to question. Whether you are being told the truth or not, you have no alternative but to wait. That is all you can do. So, I waited again. I do not even remember how long I waited.

Then one Monday afternoon, something unexpected happened.

Mondays were the days I often took my old Peugeot to the garage. After coming back from a mission, the car would usually have some mechanical issues. That particular Monday, I was at Pivot Garages. I remember very clearly, I was seated under the sun, just waiting. All the wheels had been removed from the car, because there had been so much noise coming from them. I sat there, dusty and tired, not expecting anything out of the ordinary.

At around 2 p.m., my wife came. She had arrived in a friend's car. She looked at me and said, *"They have been looking for you."*

I asked, *"Who?"*

In those days, when someone said *they were looking for you*, it was usually not good news. It meant there might be trouble. So again, I asked, *"Who?"*

She replied, *"The Provincial Commissioner."*

I paused. *"The Provincial Commissioner?"*

I thought to myself, *if I had said anything wrong in one of my sermons, it would have been the police looking for me.* But this was the PC. I did not know what he wanted with me. So, I told my wife, *"Let me take this car."* I asked the friend if I could use his vehicle while they returned with public transport, so my wife could go back to the office and I could go home, take a shower, change, and then meet the friend again outside the PC's office so he could take his car back.

That is exactly what I did.

When I arrived at the reception, the secretary saw me and exclaimed, *"Oh, Pastor, we have been looking for you the whole day."*

Without saying a word, she picked up the telephone and spoke into it, *"Pastor Mark is here."* Then she looked at me and said, *"Go, go, go,"* as she pressed a button to open the door. I walked in.

The moment I entered, the PC stood up.

"Oh, Pastor. Reverend. How are you?"

Immediately, I breathed in a little more confidence. I walked over and shook his hand.

Then he said, *"You know, you spoke with the President. The President called me this morning and told me we must give you that land. We must give it to you."*

Oh, man. I stood up straighter. I gathered more confidence and listened keenly.

I said, *"Yes. I will not tell you that I did not speak with him."*

The PC said, *"Please, have a seat. Do you have the land document?"*

I replied, *"Yes, I do. I can bring it tomorrow."*

I had kept a photocopy of the letter I had handed to Reverend Kareli. It was addressed to the President. I do not know whether the PC also had one from the President, but in those days, if the President signed something in green ink, then you knew it was sealed. Once he put that green pen on it, it was as good as done.

The PC gave me clear instructions. He said, *"Take this to the Commissioner of Lands in Nairobi."*

And just like that, the door opened.

Two to three days later, we were on our way to Nairobi. Our destination was the Commissioner of Lands office. At that time, Mr. Wilson Gachanja was the commissioner. This was sometime in the late 1980s or early 1990s.

So, we traveled. I knew I needed someone to accompany me, someone with presence, someone who would not be dismissed. There was a man in our church, a faithful member, who worked as the district works officer. His job came with unique responsibilities.

Whenever the president visited the district, this gentleman was the one in charge of laying the red carpet. He ensured the ground was clear, clean, and properly prepared. He was meticulous, commanding, and unmistakable.

He was also huge and majestic, an imposing figure. No one ignored him. He was always present at any presidential function in the district. People might not have known the depth of his relationship with the president, but they knew he was always there.

So, I chose him.

We arrived at the office.

As soon as he walked in, you could feel the atmosphere change. He was not nervous in the slightest. *"Hello, Mr Commissioner. How are you?"* He said, with full composure.

The Commissioner looked up. *"Ah, I saw you in the meeting the other day,"* he said.

They started chatting casually about a recent political event where the president had been present. They remembered details and shared remarks. I just sat there quietly, observing.

Then came the question, *"So, what brings you here?"*

Without a word, I pulled out the letter and handed it over.

The Commissioner looked at it. *"Ah, this one? Once the president has signed, we shall simply conduct our land search, and the legal procedures will follow. Eventually, you will have the land."*

That was promising. We left the letter with him. But that began another long season of waiting. A very long journey, in fact. I believe it took nearly two years of patient follow-ups and endless checking in before anything was finalised.

The process had started well. A file was opened. We were assigned to a junior officer for follow-ups. But somewhere along the way, those who had previously leased the land discovered that we were about to be granted the lease. Sensing this, they quickly rushed to renew their own lease.

So, just when we were nearing the conclusion, we were told, *"Unfortunately, the lease has been renewed. The land cannot be allocated to you."*

That was painful. But I asked, *"Is there hope for another parcel?"*

The response was simple. *"Yes. You need to look for another piece of land."*

So, I went back to the church and stood before the congregation. I told them, *"The land we were pursuing is now occupied. If anyone here knows of a piece of land that can be purchased, please come and tell me."*

Now, I only came to learn this the other day.

There were some women in our congregation, ladies who were friends with the town clerk. They spoke to him about our situation. And the Town Clerk, God bless him, told them, *"There is a piece of land here. And another one there. And another over there."*

That following Tuesday, just as I had requested, three women came to see me.

"Pastor, you were asking about land, were you not?"

"*Yes,*" I replied.

They opened a file of documents.

"*Here are the options,*" they said. "*This one is free. This one is also free. And this one too. It is yours to choose.*"

9

The Reception of Relentless Faith

So, I looked through the options. After a moment's reflection, I said, *"I will choose this one."*

It was close to the tarmac, strategically located along Bondeni Road in Nakuru. That same parcel, interestingly, is now occupied by the Seventh-day Adventist Church. But back then, it was open and available.

We began the follow-up process.

But shortly after, we were informed, *"This land will take quite some time to process. It belongs to a particular ministry. To allocate it to you, we must first transfer it from this ministry to another, and then eventually to the Office of the President. It will be a long, winding journey."*

"Can you identify another parcel?" they asked.

Without hesitation, I replied, *"Yes, I have another one."* I had anticipated this moment.

I handed them the documents for the second option.

They examined the records and said, *"This one is freehold. It is good."*

And just like that, a new journey began.

We now had to deal with the Ministry of Lands in Nairobi. This process demanded a level of persistence and consistency I had not imagined. We travelled from Nakuru to Nairobi and back, almost daily, for close to eight months.

Our routine was precise.

We would leave Nakuru very early and arrive in Nairobi by 7 a.m., ensuring that by the time the Commissioner of Lands arrived at the office, he would find us seated at the reception.

Without fail, he would walk in and greet us, *"Ah, gentlemen, you came all the way from Nakuru. Welcome. Have a seat."*

And we would sit.

We would sit there the entire day, hoping to be granted an audience. But most days, he would not spare even a minute to see us. Yet we had resolved, *we are not leaving until he leaves.*

So, we waited.

By the time he was packing up to go home, he would walk past us, surprised. *"Oh, you are still here? Come back tomorrow."*

He had no idea that we had to drive all the way back to Nakuru after that, exhausted, hungry, and unfulfilled.

But the next morning at 7 a.m., as he reported to the office, he would once again find us seated there, waiting.

We repeated that routine for months. Day in, day out.

That was our rhythm. But eventually, after much waiting, persistence, and unwavering faith, we got the land.

10

The Plot We Prayed For

The other obstacle we faced came after we finally secured the land.

It turned out that the plot was near the Assemblies of God Church. Their leadership at the time was not pleased. *"We can't have two noisy churches side by side,"* they said, *"It will be chaos with all the sound systems."*

We understood their concern. But we had no alternatives. This was the only breakthrough we had after a gruelling, exhausting journey. We were not about to give up.

When we returned to the officer assigned to us, she looked at the file and told us plainly,

"You can't be allocated this land. It's too close to another church."

That is when my companion, the friend I had gone with, snapped. Visibly angry, he thundered, *"Now tell me, since when did the Assemblies of God become a department in the Ministry of Lands? You should have told us earlier to apply directly to them!"*

The officer was taken aback. She had expected resistance. She must have known something we did not, perhaps there had been closed-door conversations with pastors and national officials from the Assemblies of God before we arrived. And now, to her surprise, here we were.

Coincidentally, we bumped into the very pastor and some national leaders from the Assemblies of God right there at the office. We exchanged handshakes, smiled outwardly, and went into the officer's office.

At that moment the officer, unsure of our connections, especially given how imposing my companion was, tried to defuse the situation. *"Why don't you go talk amongst yourselves outside?"* she said. *"Discuss with the other pastors and reach an agreement."*

We stepped outside and approached the Assemblies team. *"Let's talk,"* I told them. *"Bring your General Superintendent, and I'll call my General Overseer. Let them sit down and talk."*

I explained my position, *"I have no objection to relocating, if you can provide us with an alternative land within Nakuru that is acceptable. But we won't surrender this piece, especially since we've been through so much to get it, and we have no backup. You've already built. If anything, it's us who should be worried that our members will cross over to you, not the other way around."*

After some discussion, they agreed to look for another parcel of land for us. In the meantime, we continued with our plans.

By the grace of God, I had bought a tent from the U.S., and it was already on the high seas, headed our way.

And when the tent arrived, we had the land.

We raised that tent right there. The yellow and white tent.

And that is a whole other story.

A story of **achieving the impossible.**

11

Benches of Faith, Trucks of Favour

Now, when we started putting up the tent, it became so evident that the favour of God was upon us.

You see, when God chooses to lift you, He does not ask for permission from your background or qualifications. That divine favour, can relocate you from obscurity into visibility in a moment.

At that time, we experienced a level of favour that can only be described as supernatural.

We had barely begun the groundwork when the District Works Officer, who also served as the head of the Public Works Department, stepped in and said, *"Let's help these people."*

He spoke to the supervisor in charge of the tippers and arranged that we could use one if we provided fuel.

That was just the beginning.

We needed marram, because if you know Nakuru, you know it's dominated by black cotton soil, which is not ideal for construction. So, we needed solid ground.

The district works department gave us not one but three GK tipper trucks. They followed each other in a convoy, hauling loads of marram and concrete and pouring them at our church site.

And that is not all; we later learned we could hire a roller and a grader from the same department.

So, imagine this scenario. GK trucks, a roller, and a grader, all working daily at our church grounds.

The people of Nakuru started whispering.

"This must be a government church."

"President Moi must be coming for the official opening!"

We heard the rumours and smiled.

I had not even spoken to President Moi yet, but the perception of influence opened doors and accelerated progress.

Within no time, the floor was done, the tent was up, and the site looked like a state event in the making.

But there is more.

Before the Land, We Had the Seats

Long before we ever got the land, **I had prepared the seats.** I had a clear vision, and I knew God would make a way.

Back at the Miracle Hall in my compound *(Langa langa mwisho)*, I had bought a large pile of timber. I even purchased an electric planer and other carpentry tools. Then I brought in a young man, Tom Okang'o, a tall, passionate secondary school graduate who loved carpentry and metalwork.

Tom worked diligently.

Day by day, he crafted church pew benches with skill and joy, stacking them at the Miracle Hall in anticipation.

We had no land at the time. No building.
But we had faith.
We had vision.
And we were prepared.

So, when the marram was spread, and the tent was finally up, the very next day, the place was filled with the benches Tom had made, one after the other, rows upon rows.

It looked like a church ready to receive a head of state.

And to the public, it confirmed their suspicions. *"President Moi is surely coming."* But for us, we knew **the King of Kings had already come.**

12

The Exodus

From the Old Town Hall to the Promised Land

As we settled more into our preparations, we discovered something else that added a presidential touch.

The Public Works Department, we found out, had those iconic green potted flowers, the same elegant, beautifully trimmed flowers they used during official state functions and presidential events.

We enquired and were told, *"Yes, you can hire them, as long as they are not needed for any national event."*

Without hesitation, we booked them.

On the day of our official move, the flowers were lined up with precision, lining our new church site with elegance and flair. They transformed the place; order, beauty, and reverence all merged together. And of course, the buzz grew louder.

"The president must be coming to this church!"

Everything about the day had a presidential presence, except the president himself. But for us, the presence of God was more than enough.

We wanted the transition to be memorable. I told the people, *"We are going to walk!"*

And walk we did.

From the Old Town Hall, where we had worshipped for years, to our new home in Freehold, Nakuru, August 1992. We called it. **'The Exodus'.**

A symbolic walk.

A spiritual migration.

An emotional journey.

We marched with songs. With tears. With thanksgiving.

From *a rented hall of oppression to a land of our own.*

From dependence to establishment.

From battles to blessings.

And I made sure everyone who mattered witnessed it.

I invited the mayor, the education chairman, local dignitaries, and yes, I even invited Amos, the caretaker of the Old Town Hall.

That man gave us so many problems during our stay at the Town Hall.

Time and again, Amos withheld the key to the hall unless I bribed him. He would stand at the entrance during our service time and say, *"You know what to do."*

But I refused to bribe him.

I told him every time *"God is our provider. We will not bow to this."*

On many occasions, this man would send his children to come and lie to me right at the door of the Old Town Hall. Sunday morning, I would be there early, ready to sweep the hall before the members arrived. Then I would see the children coming, and they would say, *"Daddy amesema hayuko."* (Daddy has said he is not there.) Yet, I could see the curtain in his window shift slightly. The man was there.

Other times he would send them with a new message *"Enda ambia pastor Daddy ameenda safari."* (Go and tell the pastor Daddy has traveled.) And I would respond to the children, *"Enda ambia Daddy, pastor amesema apatie yeye kifungu ntamrudishia."* (Go tell Daddy that the pastor says if he gives me the key, I'll bring it back to him.)

So, the children would run back faithfully and deliver the message. And like a drama in a village theatre, the man would slowly rise, puff his chest, and walk with a boldness that was neither holy nor humble. He would open the door grudgingly, with an attitude, like he was doing God a favour. But I had already made up my mind. I told myself, *"I will not be bitter with this man. I will not hate him. I will not allow him to change the oil in my spirit. If he wants to walk around like he is the boss, let him. He has the key, and I need the key. But I will not bribe him, not today, not ever."*

There were Sundays when he completely refused to open. He would just walk away like we were a disturbance in his life. On such days, we held our service under a tree. Yes, under a tree. We had paid to use the hall, yet we worshipped under open skies. I looked at the people, faithful, unwavering, not one of them complaining or murmuring. That is how I knew we had something real. That is how I knew this was not about comfort. This was about God.

The Word of God does not change depending on the roof over our heads. Whether inside the hall or outside under the sun, the Word still gave life. The people still lifted their hands and worshipped. The children were even happier; they had space to run around, climb trees, laugh, and play freely. What the enemy meant to frustrate us, God turned around and used to build a stronger church family. A family that could pray and sing even when the doors were shut.

So, when the day came for us to move to our own land, I sent him a proper invitation. Yes, I invited him to our great walk of Exodus from the Old Town Hall to Freehold. And when he came, I handed him a Bible. I said, *"Thank you for being a good man."*

Not because he made life easy, but because God used him to toughen us, sharpen us, and prepare us. That Bible was not a bribe. It was a statement. A message that said, *You did not break us. You built us. And now, we are free.*

That is how God works. He takes what was meant to frustrate you and uses it to fire you up. He takes closed doors and uses them to push you into open fields. That is why I always say, *if you do not give up, you will go up.*

That day was not just about a building.

It was about faith rewarded. It was about a church that refused to be silenced, or stopped, marching into God's promises.

13

One Metre, One Family, One Vision

The day we marched to our land was not just a walk; it was a declaration. That march was our statement of faith. And it was on that very day that we broke ground for the construction of our multipurpose hall. I had sent out invitations far and wide to my fellow Deliverance Church ministers. We were not many in those days, but we had unity, we had passion, and we had faith. Among those who honoured the invitation were Bishop William Tuimising and Bishop JB Masinde, great men of God. Bishop Tuimising was the one who broke the ground.

But let me tell you something I learnt very early on. You do not just call people to a groundbreaking ceremony and present them with bare earth. No. You prepare. You set the stage. You stir up the atmosphere of expectation. So, before I told anyone, Pastor Paul Mwakio and I took action. We went to the quarry, bought a full lorry of stones, and poured it on the site.

When the people came, there was already a visible heap of stones sitting on that ground like a promise. I stood there and told them, "You can buy a lorry too. You can do something. You can be part of this." The people saw the vision was real, and the giving started flowing. We had momentum. And where there is momentum, you keep moving.

After the ground breaking, I spoke again. I said, *"This is our house. It is our foundation. So, we are going to dig it ourselves. We shall not bring strangers to do what our hands can do."* Each family was to dig one metre of foundation trench. *One metre, just one, but it would be your metre. You choose where your trench is. You dig. Then the fundi will come and straighten it and ensure it aligns properly.*

I led by example. Saturday morning, with my wife and children, we dug our portion. We did not wait for Monday. We did not wait for the fanfare to settle. By the time others arrived on Monday, they found our trench dug. The *fundis* were already there aligning it. That act alone spoke louder than any sermon. It said, *"We are building this house together."* And build we did. In record time, every family had dug their section. It was a beautiful picture of unity. And we had help; the late Pastor Moses Mwangi was with us. He knew his way around building and construction. He gave us solid guidance and practical wisdom.

Then came the real test of trust and persistence. On Monday, Pastor Paul Mwakio (may God rest his soul) and I went to the quarry again.

We wanted to understand exactly how things worked. We watched them measure the stones. We saw the stick they used. We stood there until our stones were measured, cut, and loaded onto the lorry. But we did not stop there. We had heard stories. Stories that some of these lorries would pick up your stones, offload some halfway, and deliver the rest to you.

I told Paul, *"We are not losing anything today."* So, we followed the lorry. From the quarry to our compound. And when the lorry turned back to the quarry for another load, we followed it again. We did this over and over until the lorry drivers knew, these pastors are not joking. There would be no room for shortcuts. No room for funny games. Not with us.

And that is how we started building. Stone by stone. Trench by trench. Family by family. With prayer in our hearts and dust on our shoes, we pressed on.

14

The Battle Within

Growing up, I was my mother's last-born son and an extremely quiet boy. So quiet, in fact, that at times she would forget I was even there. I would sit in silence, not for lack of words, but because I had come to believe that silence was expected of me. Everyone else seemed to have something to say, something to contribute. I was simply there. Not absent, but unnoticed.

She would serve everyone food, and there I was, sitting calmly at her side, with an empty plate and not a single complaint. It would take one of my siblings to speak up for me, *"This one does not have."* And only then would my mother turn to me, surprised, and give me a small slap, not out of anger, but with that motherly mix of love and frustration, asking, *"Why are you not talking? You should have said something."* But by then, the pot would be empty. And so, they would all share from their plates, each giving me a portion until I had enough.

The brother I followed was a different kind altogether, talkative, energetic, always in motion. He was the go-to person. If anything needed doing, they did not look my way. He would be the one sent. I, on the other hand, was often overlooked. And somehow, without realising it, I began to shrink into the background. I started to believe that maybe that is how it was meant to be. I became more of a follower, not because I lacked ability, but because I had been conditioned to think that someone else would always take the lead.

It was not until much later that I came to understand this one powerful truth. What people call you, you start to become. When they kept saying, *"This one is not talkative,"* my mind swallowed that label. I could not even speak up, because as far as they were concerned, and eventually as far as I was concerned, I was not talkative. And so, I kept quiet. Not because I lacked thoughts or ideas, but because silence had become my default setting.

That is when I learnt something that has stayed with me to this day. What you speak over someone, especially over children, matters. The words you release can build a future or break it. Many people destroy without even knowing they are doing it. They say things carelessly, and those words lodge themselves deep in the hearts of the listeners.

Because of what was said about me, I began to act it out. I became the quiet one. I became the overlooked one. And it took time, it took God, and it took purpose to break that identity. But that is where I first discovered the power of the spoken word. And now I know the quiet boy can become the voice that breaks barriers.

15

Renewing the Mind to Walk in Abundance

Every day I renew my mind by reminding myself who God is. Not who people say He is. Not who religion paints Him to be. But who He has revealed Himself to be in His Word.

When I came to truly understand the finished work of Jesus Christ on the cross, something shifted deep within me. It was not just a story I had heard growing up. It became a personal revelation. A turning point. That statement, when Jesus declared It is finished, opened my eyes to a new way of living. A new way of thinking.

You see, for years I thought that poverty was somehow part of God's plan. That struggle was a sign of holiness. But when I understood what

Jesus really came to accomplish, I saw things differently. Jesus came to deal with sin, yes, but also to deal with every consequence of sin, and that includes poverty.

Poverty was never God's original idea. Never. When He created man, He placed him in the Garden of Eden. And Eden was not just any place. The name Eden means riches, abundance and delight. That name alone tells you the kind of life God intended for man. He designed us to operate in overflow. To walk in fullness. To enjoy the good things He had made.

God said to Adam, Look at all this. All of it is yours. Eat freely. Enjoy. Just one thing I ask. The tree of the knowledge of good and evil, do not eat from it. That was the only restriction. The rest was abundance.

Adam was tested in abundance. He had everything. He lacked nothing. His test came in the middle of plenty. And yet he failed. He went for the one thing God said no to while surrounded by all the things God had freely given.

Now let us come to Jesus. When Jesus was tested in the wilderness, it was the complete opposite. There was no food. No garden. No fruit trees. No overflowing streams. Just hunger. Yet the test was still the same. It was about food. About trust. About obedience. In that place of scarcity, Jesus passed the test. Where Adam fell in abundance, Jesus stood firm in lack.

This comparison opened my eyes. Jesus overcame in the wilderness to redeem us back to Eden. Back to abundance. Back to that original design. This is the kind of God we serve. A God who does not withhold. A God who delights in blessing His children.

So, how do I renew my mind daily? I remind myself of this. I feed on this truth every day. I align my thinking with God's nature. Not a limited, stingy God, but a generous Father. A God of overflow. A God who says, I have given you all things that pertain to life and godliness.

Each morning, I choose to think like someone placed in Eden, not someone lost in the wilderness. I choose to expect abundance. I choose to walk as one redeemed. That is how I renew my mind and walk in His limitless nature.

16

Redeemed from The Thorns

One of the most profound moments in my journey of renewing the mind came through the revelation of the crown of thorns. It was one of those divine insights that turned the light on, and suddenly, the pieces began to fit.

I came to realise that in the Garden of Eden, there were no thorns. None at all. Eden was a place of beauty, pleasure and abundance. The ground responded with fruitfulness, and man lived in perfect harmony with the environment. But something changed after Adam disobeyed. Everything shifted.

Genesis 3:17–18 (KJV) speaks of this change. After Adam sinned, God said to him, *"Cursed is the ground because of you. Through painful toil you will eat food from it all the days of your life. It will produce thorns and thistles for you."* That was the beginning of the struggle. That was the day abundance turned to hardship. From that moment, Adam had to sweat and labour to receive what had once been given freely.

Thorns and thistles are not just weeds. They are symbols. They represent a struggle. They represent frustration. They represent poverty. They are a sign that the ground is no longer yielding its increase with ease. They came to make life hard. To frustrate effort. To resist fruitfulness.

So, when I read the story of Jesus being taken before Pilate and the Roman soldiers weaving a crown of thorns and pressing it onto His head, it was no coincidence. It was a divine message. A powerful picture. Those thorns were not chosen at random. They were chosen by heaven. They were a message in themselves.

Jesus wore the very symbol of the curse. He bore on His head the very thing that came into the world when man fell. As those thorns pierced His skin and His blood flowed, that was not just blood for sin. It was blood for poverty as well. That was Jesus taking on the burden that began in Genesis, paying the full price not only for our redemption from sin but also for our deliverance from lack.

You see, the work of the cross was not partial. It was complete. When Jesus cried, *"It is finished."* He was not just speaking about forgiveness. He was also declaring the end of the curse. The end of poverty. The end of struggling to survive.

But let me be clear. Just because Jesus paid the price does not mean we automatically walk in wealth and abundance. Salvation opens the door, but the principles of increase must still be followed. God, in His wisdom, placed the principle of growth in the seed. The seed is the secret to multiplication. The seed is the way out.

A seed must be sown. It must be nurtured. It must be given time to grow. Many of us pray for harvests but ignore the principle of sowing. Yet the truth remains, no seed, no harvest. It is not magic. It is not luck. It is a divine principle. God said, *"As long as the earth remains, seedtime and harvest shall not cease."*

17

The Time to Sow, The Life to Reap

God, in His wisdom, established a principle that governs the earth: *"While the earth remains, seedtime and harvest shall not cease."* It is not just an agricultural truth but a divine law, a spiritual blueprint for life, destiny, and prosperity.

Notice how Scripture says *seedtime* and *harvest*, not *seedtime* and *harvest time*. That omission is not accidental. There is a powerful truth hidden in the difference.

Seedtime is bound by time. It is a window. A moment. A season that demands action. It comes with urgency and must be seized. The farmer knows he cannot plant in any season he pleases. If he delays, he misses the window and forfeits the harvest. So, it is in life. There are seasons in which you must sow, sow effort, sow ideas, sow kindness, sow finances, and sow services. You cannot procrastinate. You must sow while the soil is ready, and the heavens are open.

But harvest... Harvest is not called harvest time. Why? Because harvest is not confined to a single moment or short season. **Harvest is a result that can stretch through a lifetime and even beyond.** Your seed may be limited by time, but your harvest is not. You may plant in a moment, but you can reap for generations.

Proverbs 11:18 says, *"The one who sows righteousness reaps a sure reward."* And Galatians 6:9 reminds us, *"Let us not become weary in doing good, for at the proper time we will reap a harvest if we do not give up."* Here again, we see that the sowing has a 'proper time', but the reaping can be ongoing, as long as we stay the course.

When you plant a seed, whether it is an act of love, a word of encouragement, a vision invested in faith, or a financial gift, you release something into the soil of life that is governed not just by seasons but by eternity. That one seed can grow into a tree that bears fruit for years. That one act of obedience can unlock blessings that overflow to your children and your children's children.

Think of Abraham. He sowed a seed of obedience by leaving his father's house. That seed, sown in time, birthed a nation, and the harvest of that obedience continues even today in every believer who walks by faith. One man's obedience in a moment created a generational harvest.

You see, seedtime is often inconvenient. It requires discipline, faith, and sacrifice. But if you miss it, you cannot reap. The harvest is endless, but it must be triggered by a seed. Ecclesiastes 11:4 warns, *"Whoever watches the wind will not plant; whoever looks at the clouds will not reap."* There will never be a perfect time to sow. You must act when God prompts, knowing that the season will not wait.

But once the seed is sown, once it dies in the soil of surrender and faith, then the heavens open and the harvest begins. And the beauty of divine harvest is this, *it is not seasonal, it is not singular, and it is not short-lived.* It continues. It multiplies. It spills into every area of life. That is why Scripture simply says *"harvest"* because God does not want you to expect a single return but an overflowing one.

So, while the earth remains, this principle will never fail. There will always be seedtime, those moments that demand our decision and obedience. And there will always be harvest, rich, abundant, unending.

The wise man recognises his seedtime and acts. The faithful man never grows weary in sowing. And the man who walks with God understands that his harvest is not just for a day; it is a legacy.

So now, every time I see a thorn, I remember what it cost Jesus to free me from the curse. And every time I hold a seed in my hand, I remember that I have been given the power to increase. The ground may have been cursed, but the curse has been lifted. My responsibility now is to work the principles of God and trust His process.

The crown of thorns reminds me that I am not destined to live in lack. I have been redeemed from it. And that truth changes how I live, how I give, and how I expect.

Because the curse has been broken. And abundance has been restored.

18

The Gift That Multiplies

I believe in my heart that giving is something I inherited from my mother. She was one of the most generous people I have ever known. And for us, in those days, giving did not mean writing cheques or donating to foundations; it meant food. Simple, everyday food.

If she was cooking and heard someone passing by, perhaps a cough, a shuffle of footsteps, or even the creak of a gate, she would call out from the kitchen, *"Who is that passing while I'm just finishing cooking?"* And the voice would reply, *"Oh, it's Monica. I'm just passing."* Without a second thought, my mother would say, *"Come, take something to eat."* She would scoop food from the pot, often before she had even served us, and hand it to whoever was passing. It did not matter if it was a neighbour or a stranger. If you were nearby and she had something cooking, you were going to eat.

My father would sometimes say to her, half-joking, half-serious, *"At least serve mine first before you give it all away."* And she would smile and serve him. But she never changed. She believed in feeding whoever needed food, and that generosity left a permanent mark on me.

Giving became part of my DNA.

So, when I got born again and started reading the Scriptures for myself, I realised something that struck me deeply; **giving is not just a good thing; it is a God thing.** It is a divine principle for increase and multiplication. You cannot get out of poverty by begging or borrowing. You break free by giving.

God's system is different from the world's. The world teaches us to accumulate, to hoard, and to stash away for ourselves. *"Get all you can and keep it,"* they say. Build your savings, guard your wealth. But in the Kingdom of God, the principle is clear, *give, and it shall be given unto you* (Luke 6:38). My mother, even without reading the Scriptures, was living out a kingdom truth. She understood that when you release what is in your hand, you create room for God to fill it again.

You do not rise by holding on. You rise by letting go.

Proverbs 11:24 puts it beautifully, *"One person gives freely, yet gains even more; another withholds unduly, but comes to poverty."* That is the paradox of giving; the more you release, the more you receive. Giving is not subtraction; it is multiplication.

So now, I find myself looking for opportunities to give. Not because I want recognition, but because I know the secret. Giving is the way up. Giving is the pathway out of lack. Giving is a seed that never dies. It may leave your hand, but it never leaves your life.

My mother gave without expecting anything in return, and God ensured we never lacked. Now I walk in that same grace, not because I am trying to earn anything, but because I understand the principle. ***If you want to receive, you must be willing to release.***

And once you learn that, you stop clinging. You start giving. And you never remain the same again.

19

From Empty Pockets to Full Purpose

Breaking through poverty was not just about money. It was a mental barrier and a spiritual hurdle as well. A mindset that had been baked into the very fabric of our upbringing.

We grew up in what many would call abject poverty. Many were the mornings we would head to school with nothing in our stomachs. Absolutely nothing. On a better day, we would take strong tea. If there was porridge, we drank it, sweet or not. If sugar was lacking, a pinch of salt would do. That was the reality. No complaints. No excuses. Just life as it was.

Then we would arrive at school and sit next to children whose pockets were packed with biscuits, bread, sweets and all manner of tasty treasures. They would pull out a slice of bread like it was nothing and eat it while you were still trying to settle your stomach. Yet something was deeply planted in us. A quiet dignity. An inner discipline. Even with nothing in our hands, we were taught not to beg.

It was not pride. It was principle.

You watched them eat. You watched them unwrap their treats. But you never asked. Never reached out and said, *"Give me some."* That is just how we were raised. And though it seemed tough, I now know it was building something greater inside us. A quiet strength.

But perhaps the hardest part was not the hunger. It was the belief that poverty was somehow holy. That the poorer you were, the closer you must be to God. We had been taught that lack was a sign of humility. That struggle was holy. That being poor meant you were more spiritual.

It took years to unlearn that.

It took revelation.

It took truth.

It took courage to stand and say, God is not glorified by lack. He is glorified by fruitfulness. He is glorified when we multiply, when we thrive, and when we bless others because we have something to give.

That shift in thinking was not instant. It was a journey. A turning of the mind and the heart. But once I saw it, once I understood that poverty was not godliness, something broke inside me. And from that day, I made a decision.

I would not bow to poverty. I would rise above it. Because I had already lived with empty pockets. Now it was time to live with full purpose.

20

The Orange That Preached Back to Me

In this journey of becoming unstoppable, I have learned that giving is not just an act of kindness; it is a supernatural law for increase. Every time someone gives, they unlock the power of multiplication. Giving is heaven's way of setting your life on a course that cannot be hindered. But there is a truth many miss, and that is for every giver to experience the blessing, there must be a willing receiver.

For years, I have taught in church that when someone offers you something, no matter how small, they are activating a divine principle. And if you say, *"No, thank you,"* you may think you are being humble, but in reality, you could be blocking their blessing. You are interfering with the divine exchange. You are saying, *"I don't want you to receive,"* without realising it.

Scripture puts it beautifully: *"It is more blessed to give than to receive"* (Acts 20:35). But it is in the receiving that the circle is made complete. Without someone to receive it, the blessing remains unsealed.

One day, I experienced the power of this truth in the most unexpected way. I had taken Mama Junior to the wholesale market in Nakuru town to buy some food items. She carried her *kiondo*, I had two baskets, and we were weaving our way through the narrow, muddy aisles of the crowded marketplace.

As we passed by one of the stalls, a woman called out to me, *"Pastor! Bwana asifiwe!"* I looked up and saw a face I did not immediately recognise. *"Praise the Lord!"* I replied. *"Pastor, I come to your church. I'm selling oranges today; bought them wholesale, selling retail. Please eat one. Just one!"* she insisted.

Out of habit, I waved it off politely. *"No, thank you. Not today."*

But she would not take no for an answer. With confidence in her voice and fire in her eyes, she said, *"No, Pastor. You taught us. You said that when someone refuses your gift, they are blocking your blessing. You said there must be a receiver for the giver to be blessed."*

I was speechless. I put the baskets down, peeled the orange right there in the middle of the bustling market, and ate it, not because I was hungry, but because I realised the power of my own words had taken root. The orange was no longer just fruit, it was her seed, her key to increase.

That day reminded me that when people are taught the Word, it transforms them. That woman did not just attend Bible study; she lived what she learned. She was no longer trying to survive; she was walking in kingdom boldness. And that, to me, is the essence of being unstoppable.

Growing up, I was raised in a culture that saw receiving as a weakness. If someone gave you something, you were told to say, *"Not at all, not at all,"* as if receiving made you needy. We were taught to give, yes, but never how to receive. And in that, the enemy quietly built a wall that kept many from experiencing abundance.

But I have learned that *giving is God's master plan to lift people out of poverty*. Not begging. Not borrowing. Giving. When we teach people to give, we give them the key to open their own doors. We move them from dependency to dominion. That is the gospel that empowers. That is what makes a person unstoppable.

Sadly, much of what is called prosperity teaching today has turned into manipulation. The focus has shifted to what the preacher can get, not what the people can become. But true Kingdom giving lifts everyone. When the people are taught the Word, they grow. And when the preacher becomes a giver too, not just a receiver, then the whole church flourishes, not just financially, but spiritually and generationally.

That day in Nakuru, the woman with the orange reminded me, when giving is understood, even fruit becomes a seed. And when receiving is done with honour, the harvest is inevitable.

The unstoppable life is not built on hoarding, it is built on sowing. On knowing that giving is not losing; it is planting. It is entrusting God with your future.

And that is how you rise, with your hands open. Giving. Receiving. Multiplying.

21

The Seed Always Knows What to Do

If there is one principle that rules every sphere of life, from nature to the human heart, it is the principle of the seed. The seed principle is not just a biblical idea; it is a law of life itself. It is a force that cannot be silenced, manipulated or ignored. Whether you believe it or not, the seed will do what it was created to do. It will grow.

I want you to understand that giving is not limited to material things. It is broader, deeper, and more dynamic. When you give love, you receive love. When you sow hatred, it always finds its way back to you. When you release encouragement, joy or compassion, they return to you in unexpected moments. And yes, when you give materially, the material comes back, multiplied, shaken together, running over.

Life itself is built around giving and receiving. You breathe in oxygen and give out carbon dioxide. The sun gives, the earth receives. The clouds give rain, the soil receives it. The rhythm of life is a divine cycle of exchange. The unstoppable are those who understand this and live in step with the rhythm of heaven.

Just like gravity, the seed principle is not subject to personal beliefs. You do not have to 'believe' in gravity for it to pull you down. It is established, and it works. The same is true for sowing and reaping. Whether you have faith or not, once you release a seed, it is out of your hands but not out of God's reach. You have triggered a system that God Himself put in place.

I remember growing up in Elburgon, a small town nestled in Nakuru County. Harvest time was always a buzz of activity. Whether we were threshing maize or beans, there was always leftover residue, the discarded bits we considered useless. We would throw them into a pit at the edge of the farm. Nothing valuable, just scraps and damaged kernels. But when the rains came, that pit would transform into a small garden. Maize would spring up. Beans would shoot through the soil. We had not planted them intentionally, but they grew all the same. Why? Because the seed always knows what to do when it hits the soil.

Even the seeds we called rubbish responded to the law of life. They were not good enough to eat, not good enough to sell, yet they germinated. That memory has stayed with me. It taught me that giving in any form is not in vain. Even the overlooked seeds, when surrendered to the earth, produce a harvest. The soil does not ask for qualifications. It receives what is given and does what it was made to do.

The seed principle is not emotional. It is not religious. It is not even always intentional. It simply is. And once you grasp this truth, you no longer wait for feelings or inspiration to give. You sow, and you trust the system God has already set in motion.

This is why to be unstoppable, we must become people who understand God's principles and adjust ourselves to them. We do not negotiate with His Word; we align with it. We do not challenge His laws; we obey them. Because when you work with the principles of God, they will work for you, just like gravity, just like the seed.

So, do not wait for the perfect moment. Do not wait to feel spiritual. Sow. Give. Love. Release.

And watch heaven multiply what you dared to let go of.

Because **the seed always knows what to do.**

Part II
UNSTOPPABLE IN THE STORM

22

Unstoppable in the Storm

Storms are part of life. No one escapes them. And if you are called to lead, especially in ministry, you must learn to walk through storms without allowing them to sink your spirit. I have faced many storms over the years, but a few stand out because they shook the very foundation of my heart.

One of the storms I have faced, and continue to see in ministry, is the storm of people walking away.

Imagine pouring your heart out every week. Teaching with clarity, feeding people with the Word of God, loving them, praying for them, walking with them through their darkest nights. Then, one day, they are gone. Without warning.

Without explanation.

And it does not end there. Some do not just leave quietly; they leave with wounds in their mouths. They speak against you. They twist your words. They rewrite your story to fit their pain. That hurts. It hurts deeply, because ministry is not a job; it is your life. It is not a performance; it is love; it is your calling.

I remember a couple I had walked closely with. We had built a deep bond. We had worked together in ministry. But suddenly, I was told they had left. They had gone to another church, a friend's church. The reason? Apparently, *"He has more revelation."*

And just like that, the whispers began. *"Mark is finished. This is the end of his ministry. People are leaving. That church won't survive."*

But from the beginning, I had learned something valuable, **my source is not people. My source is God.**

Yes, people may walk away. But God never does.

I can take you back to the year 1980, at Nakuru Christian Centre. I was still employed then, but ministry was burning in my bones. One day, three accountants, good men, mature believers, visited me. They sat in my house and said, *"Mark, we've listened to you teach. The way you handle the Word, we know God's hand is on you. It's time to go full-time in ministry. Resign. Study the Word. Pray. Preach."*

To sweeten the offer, they promised monthly financial support. *"Even if the church can't support you,"* they said, *"we will. The three of us will contribute every month."*

It was tempting. Very tempting.

More time to pray. More time to study. More freedom to minister. And guaranteed financial support, what more could a young minister ask for?

But something within me refused. Not out of pride, but out of clarity.

I looked at them and said, *"Thank you for your offer. I'm truly honoured. But if I go now because you've told me, then when problems come, I will blame you. If you fail to send the support, I will resent you. I'd rather wait until God tells me to go, because when He calls, He provides."*

They were disappointed. But I had made my decision.

I chose to wait for the voice of God. Because when you are called by God, you lean on Him. He becomes your source. He becomes your supply. He becomes your defender in every storm.

That was my first lesson in spiritual resilience. That was the storm I overcame, not by shouting louder, but by **trusting deeper**.

There will always be storms, betrayal, rejection, misunderstanding, and disappointment. But those who are unstoppable do not run from the storm. They stand in it. They anchor their feet. They lift their eyes to heaven and declare, *"Though none go with me, still I will follow."*

And when you anchor your heart in God, not in people, not in applause, not in convenience, then no storm will ever be able to stop your purpose.

I am still here. Still preaching. Still walking. Still trusting. Because God, not man, called me. And He who calls is faithful.

23

God Will Supply. The Potatoes We Never Planted

So, when those storms have come, I have stood because of one thing, **my unshakeable confidence in God.**

And honestly, I must say, I draw a lot of that strength from my mother. As far as I can remember, nothing was ever too hard for her. Nothing. She had this quiet confidence that no storm could drown us.

I recall moments from my childhood when we did not have enough for rent. The money was not there, not even close. My father, faithful and disciplined, would come home with his brown envelope, his monthly pay. I still remember the amount clearly. **Ksh 21** per month. Out of that, we had to pay rent, buy food, and pay school fees. Rent alone was 5 shillings.

Logic would say, "This *is impossible.*" But my mother never panicked. Never complained. Instead, she would simply say, *"Let's pray."*

And that was her solution. Not in desperation, but in quiet confidence. She would ask for her headscarf because, in her conviction, you never stand before God uncovered. To her, that was like standing before Him naked. Reverence was everything.

She would close the door and gather us around. Then she would pray a simple, unpretentious prayer, *"Lord, we look to You for supply. You know what we need. And we know You will provide."*

Once the prayer was done, that was the end of the problem. There was no more worry. No anxiety. She would say, *"Pick your jembe, let's go to the shamba."*

And out in the shamba, we would stumble upon potatoes that we never even planted. They had sprouted by themselves, wild, unexpected provision. We would harvest them, fill one or two *Kiondos,* and on our way home, stop by the Indian shops and sell them.

That money would pay for school. It would buy food. It would cover the bills.

God answers prayer, not just with heaven-sent miracles, but through the little things we often overlook. And that trust, that confidence, became part of my DNA.

So even today, as I face new storms, betrayal, financial pressure, uncertainty, I remember, **if I am right with God, I have nothing to fear.** If my conscience is clear, if there is no hidden sin, then the accuser of the brethren has no power. I can walk through any storm knowing **God will make a way.**

Because I have seen it.

I have lived it.

I was raised in it.

Storms may come. People may leave. Support may dry up. But God remains.

And when He remains, so do I. That is what makes me unstoppable.

24

When Influence Does Not Distract the Called

I have had the privilege of preaching during the eras of Moi, Kibaki, Uhuru and Ruto. What has kept me from being influenced or used by politicians as a political tool is my unwavering trust in God. I believe that anyone who approaches me does so because they have recognised the hand of God upon my life.

I remember when I invited Bishop TD Jakes to Kenya for the very first time, later Juanita Bynum and Eddie Long from Atlanta, and several others. After organising those meetings, a preacher from abroad contacted me directly. He said, *"I'm sure you've heard of me, and I would like to hold some meetings in Kenya. I have been told you are an excellent crusade coordinator."*

At that moment, I realised I was on the verge of being misdirected, slipping into the role of a coordinator instead of remaining a minister. I had to respond politely but firmly, saying, *"I am not a coordinator. I lead a ministry that is equally demanding. These ministers came to me because they recognised the call of God upon my life."* I have taken the same position when it comes to politics. Any politician who approaches me does so because they have seen God's work in my life, not because they can offer me something. I have no interest in their money.

I remember years ago, at the Old Town Hall in Nakuru, I would pray, *"Lord, do not open a door for me to travel abroad until this church is fully capable of supporting me. Let me never go as a beggar."* I was determined never to fabricate stories about walking twenty kilometres to church just to raise funds. My desire was to go abroad simply to preach the Word, and God was faithful.

Many ministers visited us and expressed a desire for me to visit their country. Some said they would send invitations, but once they left, that was the end of it. I never followed up, and they never sent formal invitations, although a few did return to Kenya. I was never troubled by this, because I knew God was answering my prayer.

I have always been confident in my calling. I serve God by serving people wholeheartedly and without reservation. Politicians are part of those I serve. When a politician comes to me, I do not treat them as someone special; they are simply another Kenyan who needs the Word of God.

I remember the first time I preached before President Moi. It was during a mission week at Moi University. I had been teaching every day during the lunch hour and evening sessions. They later informed me that the president would attend the Sunday service, and I would be the preacher. I prayed, asking God to help me remain focused and simply teach His Word. That Sunday, I preached without regard for status or titles. My message was centred on God's plan for salvation.

After the service, President Moi was very pleased. He kept saying, *"Kariuki, where have you been?"* Yet I did not receive even a single shilling, nor was I expecting any. I was not preaching for money. I preach because I am called to do so.

When I meet politicians, I do not view it as an opportunity for personal gain. I see it as a God-given responsibility to share His Word and fulfil His purpose in my life. I do not allow myself to become overly familiar with them as if we were simply friends or colleagues. I respect their positions, and they come to respect mine when they realise I am not seeking favours or handouts.

25

What God Thinks of Me Is Enough

From within, I have come to understand that you cannot please everyone when you minister the Word. People receive the message in different ways. Some will respond positively. Others will receive it negatively.

If you take every compliment as a true definition of who you are, you will be equally affected when criticism comes your way. That is why I made a conscious decision: what people say about me or my preaching is immaterial. I do not preach to please anyone. I preach to fulfil my calling.

So, when someone comes and says, *"That was a powerful message,"* I say, *"Thank you very much,"* and move on. If I let compliments get into my head, I may begin to see myself as a champion.

The danger is that when someone else comes and says, *"That was dry preaching,"* it could hit me so hard that rising again becomes difficult.

Whenever pressure comes from within, my first response is to examine myself. I ask, *"What part have I played in allowing this to happen?"* In every crisis, I begin with self-reflection. If I can identify my contribution, however small, it gives me a place to start. If I find that I have contributed negatively, then I seek to correct it. If I have not contributed negatively, then what others say becomes irrelevant.

I draw strength from Acts 2:1-4, 12-15 *When the day of Pentecost came, they were all together in one place. Suddenly a sound like the blowing of a violent wind came from heaven and filled the whole house where they were sitting. They saw what seemed to be tongues of fire that separated and came to rest on each of them. All of them were filled with the Holy*

Spirit and began to speak in other tongues as the Spirit enabled them.

Amazed and perplexed, they asked one another, "What does this mean?" Some, however, made fun of them and said, "They have had too much wine."

Then Peter stood up with the Eleven, raised his voice and addressed the crowd, "Fellow Jews and all of you who live in Jerusalem, let me explain this to you; listen carefully to what I say. These people are not drunk, as you suppose. It's only nine in the morning!"

That was their conclusion. From their observation, the only explanation for what they were witnessing was that the disciples must have been drunk. But when Peter stood up, he said, *"These men are not drunk as you suppose."* In other words, that was their supposition, their opinion, but not the truth.

From that passage, I learned an important lesson. Someone else's opinion of me is not necessarily the truth. It is simply their perspective.

The critical questions I ask myself are, *"How do I see myself?"* and more importantly, *"How does God see me?"*

Once I am settled on the truth of who I am and how God sees me, other people's opinions do not affect me at all. I stand firm in the confidence that God's Word is final, and His view is what matters most. That is why I have refused to allow pressure to sit on me or define my ministry.

26

Anchored in the Storm (When the Fire Finds You)

You see, there are moments, painful, heart-breaking moments, that come to test the very core of your existence. One of the hardest times in my journey was when I lost my dear pastor and his wife, Pastor Moses and Mary. It shook me deeply. I was overwhelmed, not just with grief but with the weight of expectation. People looked to me, as their shepherd, as a man of God, for answers. *But what do you say when you yourself are struggling to understand?*

I now hold dear that *I* do not have *all the answers*. And that is all right. I no longer fear saying, "*I don't* know," because truly, there are things beyond my grasp. When understanding fails, I rest in trust.

I sought the Lord for what to say to the congregation, and the word that rose in my spirit was this, *"Unless a grain of wheat falls into the ground and dies, it remains alone. But if it dies, it produces much fruit."*

I saw Pastor Moses not as one who was lost but as a seed that had been planted, one whose life would reproduce many more like him. That truth became the comfort and hope I shared with the people. In our pain, God planted a promise.

Then came another valley. When I lost my beloved wife Joyce, it pierced me in ways I cannot explain. I believed she would recover. I was confident we would walk out of that hospital together. But she did not. And there I stood, a preacher of faith, facing a storm I never imagined.

But through it all, I learned that *God's Word is not subject to my situation.* My condition does not redefine the Word. Instead, the Word redefines my condition. His Word remains eternal, powerful, and unwavering, regardless of what I go through.

Grief came. Loss visited. But they did not conquer me.

I also came to understand that seasons are part of the journey. Some seasons are bright and joyful while others are marked by darkness and tears. And when a season arrives, you cannot pray it away, you cannot ignore it, and you cannot rebuke it. **You adjust to it.**

Yes, you adjust, not in defeat, but in wisdom. You stand firm in the Word. You keep moving. You keep believing. And you keep serving. Because the season will pass, but the Word of God remains.

I draw my strength from His Word.

It anchors me.

It sustains me.

It gives me clarity when I have no answers and courage when the storm rages hardest.

This is the essence of being **UNSTOPPABLE**. Not the absence of pain. Not a perfect path. But the **unyielding faith** that even in the fire, even in the valley, you can rise, thrive, and continue with purpose.

Let the storms come.

Let the critics speak.

Let seasons shift.

I am anchored. I am focused.

I am UNSTOPPABLE.

Part III

THE FUEL THAT KEEPS YOU GOING

(BONUS SECTION)

1. **Focus is not just about doing many things.**

   It is about doing the one thing that aligns with your divine assignment. The enemy does not fear your busyness, he fears your focus. Every time I narrow my life to what God has said, clarity floods my path.

2. **Do not give equal attention to unequal voices.**

   Not every voice deserves your ear. Some voices carry distraction, while others carry direction. Learn to filter noise and amplify divine instruction.

3. **You will never live an unstoppable life with a distracted spirit.**

   A scattered mind leads to scattered results. Distraction dilutes power and steals momentum. Focus is the discipline that sharpens destiny.

4. **Some storms do not come to stop you. They come to reveal your roots.**

   Pressure exposes the foundation. If you are anchored, you will bend but not break. Let every storm prove your standing.

5. **Focus silences confusion.**

   When you are clear about what matters, everything else loses its grip. Many battles are won by eliminating unnecessary noise. Stay centred and your steps will be ordered.

6. **When you are focused, you are dangerous to every limitation that dares to stand before you.**

   Focused people cannot be stopped. Their eyes are set, and their hearts are steady. Even mountains move for those who know where they are going.

7. **People who break barriers are not always the most gifted. They are the most focused.**

   Gifts may open doors, but focus keeps them open. Focus multiplies effort and attracts excellence. Stay locked in on your vision.

8. **Focus gives birth to accuracy. Accuracy gives birth to impact.**

   When you aim with precision, your actions bear fruit. Impact is not accidental, it is intentional. Let your steps be ordered by purpose, not pressure.

9. Guard your focus the way a lion guards its cubs.

Do not entertain distractions dressed as opportunities. Be ruthless with anything that threatens your God-given vision. Protect your focus, and you will protect your future.

10. The noise of critics is a sign that your direction is correct. Stay the course.

Criticism confirms you are doing something worth watching. Do not stop to argue with spectators, keep running your race. God did not call you to please people but to pursue purpose.

11. **The fact that I am crying does not mean I am quitting.**

   Tears do not cancel your anointing. They reveal that you are still human on a divine mission. Keep moving with tears in your eyes.

12. **Some of the greatest sermons you will ever preach are not from your lips but from your scars.**

   People follow authenticity, not perfection. Your pain becomes your pulpit. Let your scars speak of survival and surrender.

13. **I refuse to let loss make me lose direction.**

   Losing someone or something dear is hard, but I still have purpose. The path may feel lonely, but the assignment remains. My direction is defined by God, not grief.

14. Every season has an expiry date. Do not build permanent doubt in temporary storms.

Storms are seasonal. You are eternal in Christ. Wait it out with praise in your heart.

15. I may not understand everything, but I know who holds everything. And that is enough.

Trust is choosing God even when life makes no sense. Understanding is not required for obedience. Let faith lead when logic fades.

16. Heaven does not need me to be perfect. It needs me to be planted.

God blesses consistency over charisma. When you stay where He has placed you, fruit will follow. Stay planted and watch growth come.

17. I choose to keep showing up. Showing up in prayer. Showing up in faith. Showing up on purpose.

Victory is in daily decisions. Champions show up even when it hurts. Keep showing up, you are closer than you think.

18. When it is hard to praise, praise harder.

Praise is a weapon, not just a song. Use it when you feel surrounded. It shifts atmospheres and shakes foundations.

19. Storms are not permanent residents. They are passing guests.

Do not decorate your house for what was meant to pass. Let the storm pass while you stand firm. Your faith outlasts the weather.

20. **The Word of God does not change with the weather.**

God is consistent, even when life is chaotic. Stand on what does not shift. Let His Word be your anchor.

21. **Unstoppable people are not superheroes. They are simply those who refused to surrender.**

It is not strength that sets them apart, it is stubborn faith. They bleed but believe. They fall but rise again.

22. **I am not perfect, but I am planted.**

Perfection is not the goal, progress is. I may wobble, but I will not wither. My roots run deep.

23. God is not looking for stars. He is looking for those who will stay.

Shining is easy. Staying is costly. But those who stay inherit a legacy.

24. The people who make history are not those who have it easy. They are those who keep moving when others stop.

Pain did not stop them. Critics did not stop them. They kept walking and won.

25. You can lose people, positions, and possessions, but do not lose your passion.

Passion fuels purpose. Passion is contagious. Keep the fire burning within.

26. My call is greater than my pain.

   Pain reminds me I am human. But my calling reminds me I am anointed. The call is still active.

27. Let people talk. Let seasons shift. Let storms come. I am anchored.

   I am not defined by public opinion. My feet are on the Rock. I shall not be moved.

28. The fact that the ground shakes does not mean the building will fall.

   You are built to endure. The architect of your life is God Himself. Stand firm.

29. **I have cried and preached. I have buried and worshipped. I have lost and still led. That is what unstoppable looks like.**

It is not easy, but it is possible. That is grace in action. That is what makes you dangerous to the devil.

30. **The day you choose to rise again is the day you announce to hell that you will not be moved.**

Your comeback is a declaration. Every time you rise, you remind the enemy he lost. Rise again.

31. **Every scar I carry is proof that I survived.**

I do not hide my scars. I wear them with honour. They remind me of battles won, prayers answered, and storms outlasted. Let your scars speak of the goodness of God.

32. **You are not finished because you failed. You are finished when you stop trying.**

   Failure is not final unless you make it your home. Dust yourself off and get back on the path. There is still more ahead.

33. **When your spirit is strong, no storm can break you.**

   Feed your spirit with the Word. Strength does not come from muscles but from meditation. A nourished spirit produces an unshakeable life.

34. **Do not make a permanent decision in a temporary storm.**

   Storms blur vision. Wait until the fog lifts. Then move in faith, not fear.

35. I do not have to feel strong to act strong.

Faith acts beyond feeling. Feelings fluctuate, but obedience is a decision. Act on the Word, not on emotions.

36. When God called you, He already saw the valley ahead.

You are not surprising Him with your pain. He equipped you before the trial came. Walk through it with confidence. He walks with you.

37. Sometimes the answer to your prayer is the strength to go through it.

God does not always take the pain away. Sometimes He adds grace to carry it. Grace is enough.

38. Do not despise the silence of God. He works in silence and shows up in power.

Silence is not absence. It is preparation. Wait in faith.

39. There is a version of you on the other side of this storm that hell is afraid of.

That is why the fire is intense. That is why the warfare is heavy. But you are coming out refined.

40. What tried to break you will become your platform to build others.

Your pain is not wasted. God turns ashes into testimonies. Your story will give others hope.

41. You do not need everyone's approval to walk in your calling.

God approved you before they even knew your name. Walk boldly, walk freely. Your assignment is valid with or without applause.

42. He who called you will carry you.

You are not alone on this journey. The weight is heavy, but His shoulders are stronger. Trust the One who sent you.

43. Do not compare your process with someone else's highlight reel.

Your journey is unique. Stay in your *lane and trust your pace. Comparison kills joy.*

44. **Even when I feel weak, I am not disqualified.**

God does not anoint the flawless. He empowers the available. Bring your weakness to Him. He turns it into strength.

45. **Delay is not denial.**

God is working behind the curtain. Trust His timing. It will be worth the wait.

46. **An unstoppable life is built one obedient step at a time.**

Big moments are made of small decisions. Obey God daily, even in the little things. Obedience accumulates breakthroughs.

47. Let your vision be bigger than your pain.

Pain screams loudly. But vision speaks deeper. Keep your eyes on what is ahead.

48. Your future is too expensive to sell for temporary comfort.

Comfort can be a trap. Growth comes through stretching. Choose legacy over ease.

49. Faith is not pretending everything is fine. It is trusting God when nothing looks fine.

Faith is not fake. It is fierce. It stands tall in storms.

50. You are stronger than what tried to bury you.

You are still standing. You are still believing. That is strength.

51. You do not have to understand everything to obey God fully.

Obedience is not about clarity, it is about trust. When you follow God's voice, He clears the path. Obey first; understanding will come.

52. Build on the Word, not your feelings.

Feelings shift. The Word stands forever. Plant your feet where storms cannot uproot you.

53. I do not chase applause, I chase purpose.

Popularity fades, but purpose endures. When purpose is clear, pressure loses power. Stay committed to your why.

54. There is power in showing up even when you feel empty.

God meets you in your obedience. He fills as you walk. Show up, and He will show off.

55. Do not pray away the process. Embrace it.

The process prepares you for what you prayed for. What breaks others builds you. Let the process do its work.

56. Worship when it is hardest. That is when it carries the most weight.

Worship is not a song. It is surrender. Praise through the pain.

57. The devil cannot destroy you, so he tries to distract you.

Distraction is subtle but deadly. Keep your eyes on God. Block the noise and hear His whisper.

58. Every morning you rise is evidence that God is not done with you.

You woke up on purpose. Let today be a day of purpose. Live it intentionally.

59. Keep going. Keep trusting. Keep building. Keep sowing.

Breakthrough belongs to the persistent. There is grace for the next step. Take it.

60. The pit is not the end. It is the beginning of the palace.

Joseph went down before he went up. You are on track even when it looks backwards. Promotion is hidden in the pit.

61. Focus is refusing to entertain options outside of God's instruction.

Options create confusion. Focus creates traction. Stick with what He said.

62. What you feed will flourish. What you starve will die.

Feed your purpose. Starve your distractions.

63. Not every open door is from God.

Some doors lead to delay. Ask for discernment, not just opportunity. Choose wisely.

64. Learn to say 'no' without guilt.

   Every 'yes' must be protected. Saying 'no' keeps your life aligned. Protect your assignment.

65. Focus makes you unpopular with the crowd but favoured with God.

   Do not fear their silence. God will raise voices that matter. Stay locked in.

66. A focused life is a fruitful life.

   Scatter produces little. Precision produces plenty. Channel your strength intentionally.

67. You cannot fight every battle and still build.

   Choose your battles. Not every comment deserves a response. Protect your building season.

68. When focus meets faith, nothing is impossible.

It is not enough to believe, you must stay fixed. Unstoppable people believe and behave accordingly. Let both align.

69. Momentum is built by consistent focus.

Little steps, repeated daily, create unstoppable progress. Keep your eyes forward. Ignore distractions.

70. The most powerful life is not the busiest one, it is the most focused one.

Busyness can be deceptive. Focus gives life direction and power. Do not just move: move *with purpose.*

About the Author

Bishop Dr. Mark Kariuki is a towering figure in Kenya's spiritual and leadership landscape. Known for his passionate preaching, apostolic grace, and unwavering commitment to the Gospel, he has spent decades igniting faith, hope, and purpose across nations.

Born into a modest home in Elburgon, his journey into ministry began in earnest in 1973 while studying at Asumbi Teachers College, where he encountered the life-changing power of Jesus Christ. That decision set the course for a lifelong mission, and he has never turned back.

In 1983, Bishop Dr. Mark Kariuki took a bold step of obedience, leaving behind his profession as a schoolteacher to pursue full-time ministry. That leap of faith would become the foundation for a far-reaching impact, not only in Kenya but around the globe. His ministry journey is marked by courage, clarity, and consistency, always rooted in the belief that with God, nothing is impossible.

Today, Bishop Dr. Mark Kariuki serves as the **Presiding Bishop and General Overseer of Deliverance Church International**, a vibrant movement of over 2,500 churches. His visionary leadership has fuelled the growth and expansion of churches and ministries across Kenya and beyond. From planting local congregations to shaping national conversations, his voice continues to guide the Church towards spiritual maturity, excellence, and societal transformation.

His pioneering spirit has given rise to several influential platforms, including Deliverance Church Nakuru, The House of Bread in Nairobi, Deliverance Church Dagoretti Junction - House Of Worship & Healing, the Majestic City Worship Centre on Kangundo Road, Ukombozi

Sacco, One Accord TV, and the Mark Kariuki Foundation, among others. Through these initiatives, he continues to equip, empower, and uplift people, spiritually, economically, and socially, demonstrating that ministry can be both impactful and holistic.

While his public ministry reaches thousands, Bishop Dr. Kariuki remains deeply grounded in his personal life. He is joyfully married to Rev. Lady Joyce Kariuki, his partner in life and ministry. Together, they shepherd their congregations and provide spiritual covering to many. He is a devoted father to three grown children and a proud grandfather, finding joy in nurturing the next generation and modelling integrity, faith, and resilience.

A pastor to pastors, a father to many, and a trusted voice to leaders across sectors, Bishop Dr. Mark Kariuki is more than a preacher; he is a statesman of the faith. His counsel is sought in both spiritual and civic circles, reflecting his wide-reaching influence and credibility. Through his books, sermons, and leadership forums, he continues to shape minds, build leaders, and speak hope to broken hearts.

Bishop Dr. Mark Kariuki served as the President of the Evangelical Alliance of Kenya (EAK) from 2014 to 2019, during which he remained a strong and outspoken voice on matters affecting both the Church and the nation. His leadership was marked by integrity, unity, and a bold defence of biblical values in the public sphere.

Throughout his ministry, Bishop Dr. Mark Kariuki has had the rare privilege of working closely, and without controversy, with four Presidents of the Republic of Kenya: Daniel Toroitich arap Moi, Mwai Kibaki, Uhuru Kenyatta, and William Samoei Ruto. Notably, during the inauguration of President William Ruto on 13 September 2022, Bishop Dr Kariuki was honoured to lead the nation in prayer, publicly committing the new Head of State to God's guidance and blessing. This moment symbolised not only a spiritual covering over the presidency but also the Church's enduring voice in Kenya's national affairs.

Bishop Dr. Mark Kariuki's life is a powerful testimony of what God can do with a heart fully surrendered to Him. His story is more than a personal journey of faith; it is an invitation to believe again, dream boldly, and live purposefully for the glory of God. His legacy is still unfolding, but its message is clear: when you walk with God, you become **UNSTOPPABLE.**

For more, visit markkariuki.org.

Other titles by Bishop Dr Mark & Rev Lady Joyce Kariuki

Bishop Dr. Mark Kariuki is a respected spiritual leader, visionary, and an Apostolic voice in Kenya. He serves as the *Presiding Bishop* and the *General Overseer of Deliverance Church International*, providing leadership to a thriving network of over 2,500 churches across Kenya and beyond. With a ministry spanning more than four decades, he has been instrumental in church growth, leadership development, and community transformation. Bishop Dr. Mark Kariuki is the Senior Pastor at the Deliverance Church House of Bread located at the KPCU Building on Haille Selassie Avenue, Nairobi, and the Majestic City Worship Centre on Kangundo Road.

He is joyfully married to *Rev. Lady Joyce Kariuki* and is a devoted father to three and a proud grandfather. As a preacher, mentor, pastor to pastors, and author of life-transforming books, *Bishop Dr. Mark Kariuki* continues to inspire multitudes to live boldly by faith and to walk fully in God's purpose. His life is a powerful testament to the reality that with God, you are truly **UNSTOPPABLE.**

www.ingramcontent.com/pod-product-compliance
Lightning Source LLC
LaVergne TN
LVHW051558070426
835507LV00021B/2649